MW00977130

Copyright © 2012 by Leandrea Hill
ISBN: 978-1475299595
First Edition.
Printed in the United States of America by CreateSpace.

Sakura: A Luvleeh Experience
Volume 1

by Leandrea "Luvleeh Poetiklocks" Hill

Luvleeh Inks & Links
Newburgh, NY

~Dedication~

I dedicate my first book to the beautiful Queen, who when I didn't see the light within she held me to a mirror- herself.
She is my guardian angel and my mother, Consuelo. D. Hill. -Mother, friend, daughter, vocal coach, teacher, community advocate, singer songwriter and most importantly my very best friend.
I honor you and your light within.

~Thoughts on Luvleeh Poetiklocks~

"Luvleeh Poetiklocks is the Da Vinci of Poetry!!"
-Gold, Poet & Host of "I M A Poet"
(Open Mic Poetry Series), NYC

"...enter the chromatic passage way to the lovely place..."
-Rick "Verbalskillz" Harris,
Author of "My Clouds Have Wings"

"...to say you've described Lee's work is a lie...to say you have experienced it is something totally different that I can accept."
-S.P., Author of "Inkspired"

"Her words are like drips of water slowly running down the side of a cup filled with wisdom, making your lips beg to drink the whole thing."
- Gemynii Evolving, Spoken Word & Visual Artist

~Acknowledgements~

I decided to open my heart and flow in this area- To those mentioned and not- you are surely a ray in my daily sunrise.

Thanks for everything.

I honor **God**, the Creator, for blessing me with a family who is forever patient with me and my gifts. I never could have rebuilt my life without God and my family. God uplifted me when I was not strong and held me when I was, each day encouraging me to write. **Consuelo D. Hill** - Mom, the days and nights that you willingly gave a listening ear and a loving hug always seemed to calm the weariest of hearts. You always supported every aspect of my creativity & life. Your voice flows through me as I write. I am humbly my mother's daughter & I love you. **Donnell L. Hill, Sr.** - You will always be my loving father. Thanks for believing in me. Each time you tell me you are proud of my accomplishments; it fuels me to keep going. **Donnell Jr.** - Big Bro- You blessed me with this gift. If you never took a C. W. class and wrote that first poem I ever read--- where would I be? My love for writing poetry comes from you & I thank you daily for sharing that moment with me- it changed my life. **Brenton** - My "Lil" Big Bro- You always had my back and kept me on the straight and narrow. You taught me about the love of God. I thank you for bringing that to light--- because He's kept me before I knew Him and ever since. To my Grandmothers-

Geraldine and Marion, you taught me the value of using ones voice. You are two very strong women. You never gave up on anything you set your minds to--- for that I strive to make you proud. I love you. To Aunt **Kim**- You teach me to live life to the fullest loving every minute! To my **paternal family**- Thanks for always supporting me. To my friend- **Barron Davis**- I love you thanks for being my number one. When I felt I couldn't continue you picked up the pen for me. Thank you, even beyond love. **Ivan Smith**- Thanks, you gave me that last push to get rolling on this book. **Jamala Milele Lott**- Thank you for your beauty and kind heart- it reflects your soul. Your photos captured the essence of my poetry. **K. Martai, Brandon McCoy, Da Champ, Dominique P.** - thanks for the collaborations. Each experience was fun & challenging. Collectively, your words compliment both Volumes of Sakura. **MistressGem**- I love your honesty & those pep talks to keep me writing! You are a blessing in my life. **Curtis H.**-*bang bang*- Thanks for your support & keep writing. **Mystalic Writings**-Thanks for always giving me the brutal truth with my writing-I admire you. **Verbalskills** –Thanks for your advice. **Gemynii**- Thanks for being my poetic sister on the path towards the stage! **Aisha**- Wilkes brought us together but friendship kept us going. Thank you for everything. You helped make this process become a successful journey. **Gold**- Your name may say you are "gold" but you are truly a platinum part of my life. I appreciate you beyond words. **Ayana Card**-Thanks for keeping me beautiful by maintaining my locs during these times; reminding me that feeling beautiful makes all the difference in the confidence of how I write. To **my readers**- May this book take you to moments in your own life where you reflect the beauty and reality of love, life and relationships through Sakura- for it truly is A Luvleeh Experience. **Spreading Unity through Poetry.***

Peace Love & Poetik Enlightenment,
Leandrea Juanita Hill
~The Luvleeh Poetiklocks of Poetry~

With each teardrop I-
gave to the heavens; God rained
down all his blessings.
- Leandrea Hill

Luvleeh

Poetically inclined to intrigue your interest
are you willing to achieve greatness?
I find peace in all things positive
take myself through elevation
where fantasy becomes reality --through motivation
I want success in all things grateful
love unconditionally, live freely, let life evolve.
Then when success carries you like the breeze
against the wings of struggle
you will over-stand what it's like to be Luvleeh.

~Preface~

This book & its sequel are composed of the years of my writing over a 5 year span 2005-2010. I always desired a collection of my work to be in publication; however it took returning home to realize the value of my work. I thank those who encouraged me to create this compilation of my poetry. I must say the hardest part thus far was cutting poems & editing those left behind to fight for literary exposure. I find that love, life & relationships are the few things that everyone can experience, though unique to each individual. Sakura-means cherry blossom, but it symbolizes those things which represent "love" & "overcoming obstacles (we) face in life". It captured everything I wanted to put into these books. Thanks for being a part of my journey. Enjoy each piece…may it bring a new blossom to your own life…

~Contents~

Acknowledgements

Preface

Contents

First Blossom: A Heart of Hearts

Second Blossom: Watering the Seed

Luvleeh Thought #9

Struggle
Children Worldwide
Gain Knowledge

Luvleeh Thought #10

Computer Sense*

Virtual Love

Luvleeh Thought #11

Death to Black Friday
Dream of a Nation*

Luvleeh Thought #12

Deception Part 1
Deception Part 2
Pursuit of Love

Luvleeh Thought #13

Squalid Woman
Her Sickness
Tobacco Burn*
Fortress of Solitude

Luvleeh Thought: True Story

Ghosts of the New South

Luvleeh Thought #14

Invisible Conversation
America-Land of the Homeless-with Da Champ*
I Ache

Luvleeh Thought #15

According to Church Folk*
Brrrrat Tat

Luvleeh Thought #16

The Poet Called

Blaq Majik*

Necessity to Write

Sequence*

Luvleeh Thought #17

Gun Shots
Blind Theories*

Luvleeh Thought #18

The Hunted

Third Blossom: The Stories Untold

Sakura Thoughts

Who is Luvleeh Poetiklocks?

Appendix

***Please note all starred pieces
can be found in the Appendix for further explanation***

~First Blossom: A Heart of Hearts~

Photographer Leandrea Hill

A Heart of Hearts: *Love is more than a word that comes and goes; as the song says; love is the depth of the soul that knows itself, before self knows God or Creator. It is more than a feeling- it connects man to woman; man and woman to child; man and woman to nature in and of itself; man and woman to the unknown- it is the glue to life. It draws people in and wraps them. It is passionately a gift that we create by showing the beauty of a giving heart, an open mind and a receiving soul.*

Know love for all its worth in self; world; higher connections OR even overcome pain with love. Love is not a game; Love is created to draw me to you--- and you the same. We must be conscious of all we draw into self-what we think and feel reflects us, so reflect love. Allow your heart to be free- share in love. This section deals with the joys and pains of love even its counterpart...lust.

Luvleeh Thought #1
The beauty of love comes when one knows self, over-stands
others- and reaches for more.
-Leandrea Hill

Awakening

I am awakening---
Changing my old environment,
from a busy city
to a mountain village on a lake,
where black birds dive into the green
acreage, is invigorating

I am awakening---
Returning to live in mom's house
rent free- no more billings,
on the second floor, facing the east,
feeling the sun against my cheek
set daily, is rejuvenating

I am awakening in this stimulation

I am awakening---
Taking the time to focus
on weight loss dieting,
shedding fat cells to fit a new frame
a shopping spree is soon to be
this body, is more energizing

I am awakening---
Beginning a new career
as a bold new writer,
capturing the stories in my mind
creating imaginary
reality, is enlivening

I am awakening in vitalization

I am awakening---
Forgiving the man that left
to sit in a steel cage
trapped from his own society
he chose to rob himself blindly
no more fearing him, is my healing

I am awakening---
Praying to my Father God
to guide me on my path,
no more distractions
sovereignty for He is my king
joy in seeking Him, is uplifting

I am awakening in my elevation.

I am awakening---
Teaching other women love
Doesn't hurt, [poetry
is morality--therapeutic],
age embodies my mind's wisdom,
understanding, is inspiring

I am awakening---
Learning the differences
between trust- and lusting
where loyalty is most important
not just sexual deviance,
my awareness, is enriching.

I am awakening to my education

I am awakening---
Lighting the poetic trail
vers libre like flashes
of radiant metaphoria
rhyme scheme is the meter'd dirt road
my literary growth, is shining

I am awakening---
Forming an alliance work,
revising a poem,
enhance it like energy saving
light bulbs-long durability
turn on the switch to start reflecting

I am awakening the inner connection.

Winter

* Barron Davis & myself

*Two months together
Penetrating our union
Patience creates love.*

All I Want Is

All I want is...
The only thing that will open me up
And relax me down;
Those proliferated quakes from your touch
In the morning.
The Sunday kisses that carry me to Monday nights
Waiting for you to return...
Like rain droplets on dry land
All I want is...
Unconditional cares
In compatible ways
I want hips to rock to mental beats
As you talk me out of my panties
With cranium stimulants
Degrees of tension
Pecks that apperceive,
Each- desirable stroke- of my fingertips
All I want is...
Trips around the world to see villages and cities
From mountain tops and valleys
So I can relate the visual to what I feel
When you are inside me
See I—
Am lost in your pass-port
Dock me
Tie me to posts and lock me
Floating in a sea of charismatic elations
Cause you are my captain
I- your first mate
We can set sail in the night...
Let coast guards track the whereabouts of location
When we shipwreck from water rotations
Sucked into hurricane
From pre-existing weather disturbance
You got me in turbulence
Your longitude
Finds my latitude where we divide seconds
Into tenths, hundredths, thousandths
Like my yoni- gasms...
All I want is...
Conversation in the next day

Where we dialogue about making primitive decisions
To become motivations, uplifting
Those who intercede into our matrix
Knowing life is truly what you make it
And we are making endless possibilities
Through research and fertility.
Fertilize creativity
Develop new ways to reach infinity
Above the cerebral affinities
Higher learning in universal proximity
For we stand outside the box;
Sharing in discussion where ideas
Become more than thoughts---
All I want is...
Loyalty, to yourself so you will over-stand
How to be more faithful to me-
So my actions become your reaction
But it is our chemistry
            This is -what I believe...
When you are forgiving
            When I learn to listen
When we share in giving
            No one is stuck on blaming
When we live without shame and
            Poly is the love we claim---
Multi unit –
One knowing
That true being
Comes from recognizing
Our differences make us all the same
Ionic bonds of efficacy

Do you see?
We are more than what we want
We have what we need
            Reflections of his and her
Reformation of yours and mine
            Recreation of time and space
Re-living in a new dimensional truth

All I want is...You

Luvleeh Thought #2
Sometimes two must overcome shattered hearts to see the
beauty in love.
-Leandrea Hill

Love's Requisition -with K. Martai Richardson*

"I am ready for love…
Why are you hiding from me?---
I'd quickly give my freedom
…To be held in your captivity ---
I am ready for…"

…Love…
So seek and you will find
As I have found
The key to unlocking my heart
Bound by self-imposed captivity
It chose to be freed by you-
I am ready for…

The chance I needed when you stopped to listen
You took time to hear the words my heart cried out
Rather than the thoughts of others
You didn't pass judgment
You only questioned my love
And I told you-
I am ready for...

More than I thought you could handle,
But you answered my love
With doubts dismantled,
I am a man reassembled
By the second half
To an incomplete soul-
You revealed mysteries
That I couldn't hide
I saw it in your eyes---
The lift to my rise,
The support for my falls,
Pain cried out,
And you responded to my calls…

Taking in all of my past transgressions
So that I may heal
Showing me what it means to have unconditional
Blissfulness
Yes this is what you taught me ...
When you asked me to open-

Doors that took years to close
Before you, there wasn't another,
For you have taught me love
Like none other
Gave me solidity, where confidence is the gain...
Subtracting pain
You added us to trust-

You broke down walls that took years to build
Could love be so gentle?
For all I knew before you was pain
But you chose to teach me
Gave me wisdom, where joy is the gain...
You wiped I's with us
And took me... to oneness with you
For that my love is true...

Harmonious souls on the same accord,
Your love was over-poured
Yet, I sought more-

Supporting my creative endeavors
As though my thoughts are your own
We have grown-

For that my love is true---
I can entertain thoughts-
That we share as our own
To you, my heart is loaned...

I learned to let go
My trust embracing
All you have to offer,
Like the heart of your treasure
Like the strength of your presence,
And your sexual pleasure...
And your sexual pleasance...

No need to dwell on anything else
But your essence
For in it is the light of many kings
I feel safe within your kingdom
Can't you see?
In you I've found complete
Security- in being me.

To accept you,
My essence is honed
For what is a king
Without a queen to share his throne?
I see as clear
As your light in my path
I was ready for love-
Before you even asked

"So tell me what is enough;
To prove I am ready..." For Love.

Portal to My Soul

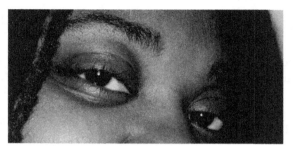

*My Eyes

Portal to the soul;
Lies deep within third eye's key;
Walk into new light.

Voluptuary Goddess

She is a voluptuous deity.
Her curves take on direction
Expanding hands as they do the mind
Her supple skin reminiscent of billowing clouds,
Have men floating on nine.
She has intellectual motivation
That encourages concentration
Satisfying cranium stimulation
Seven ways to heaven- with lips locking,

Hips rocking, side... to side
Eyes drawing an illustration of beauty
Follow the directions to paradise

She has control, enthralled by what she doesn't lack.
Healthy woman, ass sits on back...
Her rack it matches
Stacked, yes she is, plus size Goddess,
Luscious, delicious Yoni
Like watermelon, has men spitting seeds.
She triggers what safety couldn't hold-
Misfiring hitting pedestrians like antique wishes
Making childhood dreams come true.
Her tresses like a sundress in spring
Scent resembling *milk and honey*...
Leave their strong bone growing,
Draw tongues in curves
And know what home cooked tastes like
Fresh as glazed ham, mac n cheese, collards
Cabbage, rice, corn bread, black eye peas
Two people sharing the thanksgiving of Holy days
People's breath she takes away,
Blessed is this woman that makes men say
"One woman is all I need",
"Can't let her slip past me."
Voluptuary Queen, this rare woman is worthy.

Luvleeh Thought #3
With you time lingers inside mystery; fantasizing about reality because we live in our dreams.
-Leandrea Hill

Daydream

Day...Dream of the touch
Last left against my side
You had me riding words
Sprinkled fairy dust,
I was your midsummer night;

I bit my lip just a little,
Repeatedly... touched
Here...   there...
Inner thighs felt rapid waters
Rafting into my daydream, baby

There is nothing we can't do
Light reflecting into my consciousness
No longer telling
If it is my hands or yours

Tingling chills down my legs
Not of earthly creation
My imagination is taking flight
        High pelvis...
            C and F
        S   A
    I   L
  R   L
        rise and fall
        ...down...
Hey baby...let's get away
Meet me in dreamland.

Sunshine Black

His day starts when mine stops
    Good morning Sunshine Black.

I feel connected, even in the absence of his existence
My moon keeps him balanced
    Elegant yet valiant ---sunshine
Complimenting the delicacy of my living
He's rhythmic to my breathing, so in tune-
    Mahogany noon...
The colors that exude from him
All reds, oranges and blues...the sun
It's black. See his black sunbeams; I know he shines.
My eyes are blind. Through him my spirit sees God.
Just knowing he is my black piece of sunshine
    He's mine...
All I perceive is he- near me
Though in two different eternities...
His day ...My night...Meeting at cusp of eve
Where we join together and share sky...
Gives knowledge as he teaches me about light

Who is this Black Sunshine?
He is my black brutha fighting the struggle,
    My revolutionary hustla
He is my black brutha the father forgotten
    Baby mama's complaining he ain't nothing
        But he works for all he's got
He is my black brutha locked in the black {w}hole
    The only thing keeping him up-- is the black soul
He is my black brutha I am his earth
He respects me like his mutha-birthed
Black brutha educated; Black brutha non- duplicated
Black brutha his love is anticipated
He over-stands the instrumental;
He is the heart of ancestral; He is original
He is eternal; His life -there is no slack
He is my Sunshine Black

Luvleeh Thought #4
Change poor self esteem into Pour self esteem, fill yourself
with love, joy and all wondrous energies that will exude
your beauty.
You are light- Shine.
-Leandrea Hill

Love Struck

Love struck gold when ring popped face
Brought tear to blackened eye
As screams began to fade
Ignoring the neighbors cry to *hush that noise*
She dragged out the remainder of her tattered body
As hands grabbed for chains
Door blocking path to safety
He took back what he gave her in lashes
Whipped like slave to master
It was his woman anyway---

She obeyed and obliged
As child stood by side and watched man
Who was not father, beat out his mother's life
Hush it up child-don't you cry'
Gave child pieces of what his childhood lacked
Or had too much of in fact
As cycle of abuse took front seat, as love took back

See face swollen from bat---
Her black skin now shades of purple, deep reds, and blue
Like she was painted in the colors of his pain
Now drawing out life
In misery--- Slain
Laying on cold wooden floor
Panels soaking in her crimson flushing fluid
Leaving her body more convulsive
Than she ever thought she could flow
Conducive shivers--- and let go

Child runs near but kicked back, broken and fallin'
Fatherless now motherless orphan
Left stranded to the blow his mother took
For being too afraid to be alone.

Knowing When

*Me

Know when to let go
Thinking of him wrecks the mind
Do not lose control

Daylight Savings *

Clock ticks fast and I ain't lasting, you gon' have to pass
Weary days are no longer accepted in my path
You were once a present source, but now you are my last
Tick tock, tick tock...

Tick tock
...tick
......tock

I took to many days to try to get you to understand I
Am no ordinary woman
I remember when you had nothing
And I stood by your side
Like state farm you crash coursed the car
Killing both you and our relationship
I would cut my days in half
Like empty carcasses in nameless graves
Just to make space for you-
To tell me you don't have the time
It's amazing how 24 hours are in a day
But you, don't have the time;
168 hours and I just ask for a minute
Damn, what the hell did I see in you?
I saw what I didn't in self
Self hate and destruction,
I looked at you as my worst reflection
No blame because I was given the lesson
Don't be a mat if you don't like walking
Think on it...
Left me cussing you out because I couldn't stand up
I tried to see the problem as a challenge
Like you would really change
But the change was needed in me

Tick tock
....tick
.......tock
How many times does it take
For you to tell me I am just too big?
Or maybe you don't like the vocab' that I spit
See, I have knowledge over what you try to bring me

You can't take me down; I just let my love run round
Naïveté not accepted; I have graduated
No need to dwell on how I got here, because my present
Takes my past and will not duplicate it
Like photo copies, you are carbon; I the original
I dispose of you like VHS videos
Need I say more...No, stop wasting my time...
Don't call back...I won't fall back
Why are you chasing my whereabouts now?
I rotated the clock forward
Daylight savings time...
I need the energy of sun to burn out any discrepancies,
Like a sundial, I slowly let nature take over me
Showing direction, I am not misguided
So... I let the clock tick
...Tock
Tick tock
...Tick...

Clock ticks fast and I ain't lasting, you gon' have to pass
Weary days are no longer accepted in my path
You were once a present source, but now you are my last
Tick tock, tick tock...

Tick tock
...Tick

Luvleeh Thought #5
Desires of the heart carry me into blissful reality.
-Leandrea Hill

Eternal Bliss

It's a physical desire to be with you,
Separate time and make the second
Respect the minute, so you and I
Can be wrapped in forever

You draw in my breath and exhale my pain,
You got me smiling an unknown joy
Where your invigorating touch
Causes laughter to fill the void

You and I; are dancing among cirrostratus,
The music of a harmonious breeze
Sings sweet melody, the verse to our beat...
Blowing kisses at your flaming heart,
Thanking you for your light
Shadows now carry a glow

Confident in your abilities to know
Each curve; Each nerve; Each ...
Yes, you leave me wanting more
I taste your couverture,
Yes, as you savor my nectar
You and I; Together, mix the sweetest elements on earth

Baby, Yes...I... Want... You
Deep within my soul,
Let your seed plant itself in me
Our hearts nurture this moment
For as you give me time, I give you forever.

You and I; Together, we are eternity
Please... don't- let-- go
I love you.

Luvleeh Thought #6
Take in the ambiance of poetics; as they trickle into
SOUL, take in words and exhale the VISUALS.
-Leandrea Hill

Poet

Poet, you are sweeter
than the molasses you pour into me
I drizzle your words in my thoughts
like early morning breakfast
I am your eggs, grits, and pancakes
The elements of southern love...

You take in all of me and give out spoken words
Lyrically you deliver airwaves,
I'm riding the mellifluent vibrations
Your voice sends through my soul
Yet you don't even know me...
I stare at the stage drawing all of you in
Your metaphors burn through flesh;
Your words singe. My body wants to give in
Staring... at you Poet-

You can say simple haiku's or long drawn out epics
Wanting your words to create epileptics
Damn Poet... I never thought words could be so despotic
Make me slave for your po-erotic-isms
Placing verbs to adjectives
Can I be your Pronoun?
Cause I'm all for getting down...

You got this thing about you...

But my words fall to deaf ears...
It's my thoughts that want you to control
In the back seat of the café
Watching words smoke out your mouth
like burning cigarettes...

Poet, you have me dropping dollars, snapping fingers
Whistling out like- "Yes, Mr. Poet"
But truth is...
I want to have you linger like your words...
On my lips.

Late Night Loving

At the jazz club
A night out for self
Time to shake the stress
      No work. Just play, like the bass.
The lead vocalist
Scatting a riff or three
Piano man staying in tune with
Her *be- dow-dee* and the drum kicks
      Kak ti-kat, Kak ti-kat

My eye catches his
I take a sip of Merlot
As I feel the beat of fantasy
      The spot lights against his face
He's on stage for me-
The vibes are strong
Conducting melody
      Zi zooby-dee, zooby-die, dooby-doe

His toffee colored skin
Delectably draws me in...
Smile like cream, I am whipped
      Midnight strikes the clock...
And the band slowly plays into the next set
Saxophone solo conjuring my soul

I walk to his seat
He looks at me, knowing the thoughts
I want to unleash
      "Yes, I would love to dance my queen"
Less- speech- inverted conception of his kind gesture
He takes the lead and guides my step
Allowing his hand to find the curve
      In the small of my back...
The saxophone now tells our stories...

His Hershey kissed eyes...
Take me into a sassy groove
We are in tune
      Kak ti-kat

Taking time to let our feet massage the floor
With twists, turns and dip
Wind my hips to his

Yes--- I want his lips.
Honey smooth ---leave a drop on my tongue

>   *Dee dow... Be bop lee*
Tap against my imagery
As I imagine he and me
Dancing in covered satin...
>   Finding his way around my floor...
>   Slick and ready to feel his steps

Jazzy soul star he is
And I am in his galaxy
>   Kak ti-kat
He can move
See the grace of his feet
Leading. This is my night.
He whispers in my ear
>   "You are beautiful, brown sugar...
>   I wonder do you taste as sweet..."
Leaving me, syncopated in his cross rhythm
Inner voice screaming for his fusion
I-am lost in this late night loving...

It's alright, I know that loving he
Only in this moment
>   Will free ... the jazz... in me...
Damn, he is sexy
I want to know his polytonality-

>   *Die doo-bit-lee zoo bit doe,*
>   *Zee doo-bee doo-bee-die*

Late night... recap as he caresses me with musicality.

Luvleeh Thought #7
It is those things that fill our soul
that nourish the flesh.
-Leandrea Hill

Soul Filled

* *Jamala Milele Lott,* http://confessionsofa.webs.com/confessions.htm

Full figured Goddess
Bends the imagination
As she fills the soul.

To You*

I want to **make love** to you

A thousand ways past reality

Without even **touching** you

I want my **words** to take you from

Quantum physical – to metaphysical

Open your mind

Forget the past heartache

Trust ---

Together

Righteously

Uniquely

Steadfast and True

For **I** will **give mind body and soul to you…**

Pleaser
Her lips locking like locs
…around tip
……slide his girth deeply
into throat…

He feels her thoughts
as she takes it in…
rippling tongue like waves of emotion…
passionately,
swallowing his creamed honey.

Luvleeh Thought # 8
The night holds the key to Pandora;
will you unlock for a peek?
-Leandrea Hill

Night Out

*My Sisters Amber Milliner & Jeneta Tunnell

Music beats the wall
Dancing precariously
Drinks, lights, sweat-Good times

Morning After Volume I

Wake up, crust still in eyes, to unfamiliar bed.
She turned to him and him to her- nothing said.
What happened, bounces off walls in the sun cut room
The light, a two edged sword; How did they get here?

Late night mixing with his and her kissing,
The drinks were half the fun.
Hopped in rides; 'Cause the grind
Was enough to unlock Pandora

They entered right in—full of tropical sin
Firm melons, a ripe plum ass;
Coconuts and plantain; Hungry for bliss
No first names and no last

Sharing the one thing they had to be freed,
Liberated into the canny sheets
Because life at the moment was careless-
He tore at her dress; she tore through his chest;
They got to give all they stored deep,

Natural springs and hot water holes,
Refreshment in the savory drink;
She needed his licentious touch linked
As night held their voracious moans

So why be startled when eyes open?
Light giving off details to what was chosen.
The covers tell the story;
The looks confirm the journey
They can't turn back now---

So what to do but continue the chapter-
Next week it's the sequel- Vol. II. Morning After.

The Storm

You ...are the drip
Left- from a summer rain
      Canvas my... window pane
          the mirage, of fogged glass

Though the eye, has since passed
Nimbus clouds, have poured out
      Yet remain. A sigh escapes my lips
My heart reflects...the storm

Trembling thunders that thicken the heat of release-
      The electricity, fires-
          Dancing; in the distant meadows
      Lighting flashes of what lies in the darkness
          The echoes of my moans-
      Trees sway
    To the motion-
Of strong winds blowing
    My leaves
Tangle me in your vines
      Let me swing- into your canopy

Beat. The shivering stick-
Against. The ceremonious drum-
I will. Be your sacrifice-
Tingling the tongue
      Towards tantalizing remnants of a tear
That escapes, as you- take in, my convection
      Feel, cyclonic rotations, explore my cape-

Lost in derechos
Moisture convergence
Outbursts of pulse storms
From a blissful and powerful encounter
Storm scale
Record high
Licking up my virga
While rotating wall clouds
A tornado burrows within-
Together
We
Micro-
BURST.

Love In Galactic Paradigm

Space opens up
So time can sift my thoughts into stars
And planets, orbit my words
As poetic constellations form
Astrological signs,
Which predict... your every move

Prophetic in the seasonal transitions
Forecasting your destination
Determine emotion; thoughts; creation
Sun becomes center to my universe
Although only a piece of my poly- orbital space

Chasing the moon's light
Through what we see as darkness
The reflection of my luminescence
Building pyramid's in the atmosphere

Outside the earth's troposphere
Wind becomes a movement of the past
As the air element takes in the breath of subsistence
In a mystical inhalation of your oxygen
Fill my lungs with your passion.
Compliment my hemisphere

I am acronychal;
Become whole in rising
Allow aether to manifest our connection
I am Libra hot and moist by nature
Fruitful in my gifts
Presenting them, wrapped in love

Chemistry deeper
Than the penetration of the speed of light
To a naked eye
You are the vital force to my life

Living as Alchemist
Studying the alchemy of my existence
You know each element of my vital-ism

Elongation of axis
Allow planetary interaction
Un-wandering stars begin to move
Following the dance of our sacred geometry
Watching the synchronicity of cosmic energies

My lunation
Formulating the creation
Of your desire to come closer
To our evolution
Sensitivity striking cause for action...
Take in my orbital –synastry
Compare your sign to me

We are compatible in every layer of time
Space giving right to release
Reception of your polarity
Absorbing all qualities of psychometry

Above the earth
You take me...
Our spirits in the heavens
Melodically play
We become more than man and woman
We become more than energy
We become more than chemistry
We become the unknown
We allow others to see
The shedding of our love in galaxies.

~Second Blossom: Watering the Seed~

Watering the Seed: *Situations we go through, experiences we have with others or those things which we don't acknowledge in essence represent life-our seeds. Struggles, actions, the simplicity of nature; these are all seeds to life. Never let those things that happen to you in life take over your overall drive to be greater in this world.*

I've learned never to fear using my voice to speak on matters of importance. Poetry is my outlet, it is my mic. In my workshop, "Finding Your Voice", I teach the importance of using your voice in life. When you speak out against those things which alter or affect your life, then you are taking action. This can be speaking out- internally, such as dealing with self or externally such as towards the public.

Every life experience is not a new challenge; rather a new adventure towards becoming a greater person. Enjoy every turn, every person you meet along the way, for in these experiences there are answers to your next phase of life. There is a lesson to learn; be sure you are taking notes. This section speaks towards the situations that may occur throughout one's life and gives those experiences a voice.

Luvleeh Thought #9
Adventures may lead to experiences where only you can be heard; speak up, speak out and allow your voice to hit the airwaves.
-Leandrea Hill

STRUGGLE

i

    STRUGGLE
        KNOWING MY SOUL
            CONNECTS TO YOURS
                FREELY SEEKING WISDOM
                    IN YOUR SOLITUDE

i

    STRUGGLE
        KNOWING THAT YOU
            ONLY OPEN TO APPEASE
                MY LONESOME WAYS

i

    STRUGGLE
        BECAUSE i WANT MORE
            THAN YOU ARE WILLING TO GIVE
SO, FOR MY LOVE-

i

  S
   T
    R
     U
      G
      G
       L
       E

Children Worldwide

Children starve worldwide
As obesity rate climbs mountains
Like the bungee cord belt size of elastic pants

Children are homeless worldwide
While families can't find each other
In multi-level mansions
Complaining about what room to stay in

Children are parentless worldwide
Orphaned, left to raise self and are defenseless
Yet, the battle never ends

Save our Children worldwide
'fore there are no more Children to save.

Gain Knowledge

What will it take? What will it take?
The cry of a teacher trying to reach students
The youth failing to recognize the effort
put into teaching; they took the seat and flipped it
still wondering why student just called you a *Bitch*
The children's minds are lost in the hype
The hype of vixens and their hip hop video dreams,
lost in the idea that becoming a rapper
Will change everything
lost in the idea that school is for lames
Yet you have teachers with salaries
less than livable in this Hollywood glamour society
of rich athletes and over paid actors
Then we wonder why there isn't enough teachers
Or money to fund the programs needed
To educate our children
Folks going around neglecting their education
for fifteen minutes of fame

What will it take? What will it take?
To get the teachers the credit they deserve
for taking the wisdom of the world
simplifying it to be taught and giving it to our youth
What will it take to get you to realize that school,
Though you may hate it is the only way to success,
Can't have people taking all your tests
getting the money that you deserve
Educate yourself; don't waste yourself
Learn to mature; for your degree speaks
Learn from teachers who care to show you
What it is- to Gain Knowledge.

Luvleeh Thought #10
She found solace in the virtual affection,
so she stepped into his matrix.
-Leandrea Hill

Computer Sense

Natasha L. Guy

Shift the control key
Enter the backspace; pause break
Esc the spacebar.

Virtual Love

I can't feel your touch…
But I can see your face…

I can't taste your kiss…
Or smell the fragrance off your neck…
But I can hear the coo of your voice…

Yet, I still love you---

For you exist in the now …
The virtual…
I wait for the buzz of your words to grab my
attention

Never met …
Yet, I am in love with you.

My hands become yours nightly…
I see you in my dreams…
I taste the flavorful pleasure of your lips
I smell the aroma of love burrowing off your
body
I hear your voice ringing through me…

Yet, we only had one phone call…

Skype; yahoo; we are always connected…
We are simply in two realms
the now and virtual-reality.

Luvleeh Thought #11
Being enslaved to the dollar; enslavement of the modern mind
-Leandrea Hill

Death to Black Friday

We get caught in the hype...
Spending money for things,
In a month, will be over and done.
Children in third worlds are forgotten,
We cast them out
Like we do the meaningless items that we possess
I wonder where our values have gone.
The day when we cared about what happened to our neighbor

Acting out what media says we should be
Going broke for falsified real-a-lie-ties; realities
Did you catch the cries beyond the noisome pestilence?
The babies die out in silence.
Master, Visa, Gold, Black, Platinum; Debt
I am indebted to helping those who have not
But folks still rather pay for overpriced denim
And wonder why they can't afford the simple things
Lights off, cars shining, riding E-
But still bust in Wal-mart doors for a day.
They call it black for a reason.

Black as death,
Those dying from the greed of materialistic things
Black not like me,
For black as me knows the struggles of yesterday
Black as me knows, there are better things in this world
Money can provide: That a small mouth fed,
Is worth the same old clothes I wear from years ago
It understands having one meal less,
Sending it to the child who cries to mama,
"Where is the next meal coming?"
I will never spend another dollar on Black Friday
Instead, I will

Mourn those who still fall victim to its blow
Swinging out faster than swiping cards
Faster than the cashier pops open his register
With filthy green
Currency, 25 percent cotton
Interesting, we once slaved for this cotton;
Yet now we still are
Americanized red and blue synthetic fiber whips crack air;
Can you hear?

I will thriftily give back to my community
Through my creativity
Provide foods and clothing to those who are needy,
Like I once was in my not so distant past...
Do not judge what things I had or have
Poverty lasts only because we choose to put our dimes
Into dying items
We would do better investing in caskets
How did we get here?
Stop empowering the ignorance
By spending foolishly.

Dream of a Nation*

We know where we've been
We know where we're at
But how do we get to the place we want to be
> For "*Procrastination*
> *is the assassination*
> *of destination*"
Set us free of discrimination

Our mission---through legislation
Emancipate our proclamation
Execute the nation
From oppression
Aggregation of many races fight for unification
No allegations for change-
But realizations through declarations
That we can make a difference

Using the format of the our four fathers
God, Spirit, Universe, Energy
This created a connection
That birthed our divinity
Not to be held back by assumptions
Or aggravations

I am a woman--- yes
But I represent those who stood before me
Scott-King, Shabazz, Baker, Clark, Hamer, Jones
Whose words, did not go unknown

We can stand together; provoke Wall Street to listen
Stop taking our youth and grinding them into the system
No child left behind but every child lost
For they're missing—education
Can't read or write
But can stack numbers and cook coke;
Chefs in the kitchen
Only to flip it back to a community that's given them nothing
Cause government controls the distribution

Sally Mae trying to make up the difference
How many of us are jailed
How many in prestigious institutions
Left out of organizations
Spark up those flames and pay attention
Get high off the knowledge of our precession
Grab a mirror –Look deep into your reflection
This is the one who can make the difference in your recession
>   No more regression,
>   No more regrets
>   No more indolence---

Speak then act
Act then react
Wait long enough to know you have made an impact
Like contagious swine flu epidemic
Not just 28 days
A month counting a weekend in January
When we don't celebrate a King on his actual birthday
Understand the mockery
You are only a clown if you follow the black face parody
Know your history Revolutionary
Cause it's you who gives the truth to the blinded shepherd
So sheep don't follow waywardly

Preeminent antecedents' intrinsic power
Is encoded in our dna...
Fight for justice
Live for peace
Take action today
Use third eye to see

We know where we've been
We know where we're at
Freedom will give us the place we want to be.

Luvleeh Thought #12
Only you can remove the blinders to deception.
-Leandrea Hill

Deception Part 1

You try to define the deceiver;
When the only lies that are told
Come from your mouth
I just decided to trust them
When they raped my ears;
The years, I spent trying to decipher the truth
I was taught not to trust men from their actions
Because their words were always void
I was taught to protect self from the harsh realities
That my sex was worth more
I was taught to pray and give thanks to God for life
But I was never taught that life is easy
So I had to go out and find self in the streets-
I was deceived.
The black hole sun has covered the light---
Sucking in the lies
The lies---I was taught that you were to protect me
When I was hurting
Seeing the death, knowing it was the only escape.
Burning flesh scorn the floor,
Smoke twirling around my feet
Drowning my fears, back hard to the sand, falling-
Cursed crucifixes try to exorcise my inner demons,
When really it's them.

Deception Part 2

Burning the woods of lust,
Exhausted in the suffocation
Smoke engulfs the life,
Phoenix way to beginning
Adam, Eve conceptually exist
Like the rest of those told in books.
Nothing is ever what it seems.

Deception.

Pursuit of Love

She trusted him in the gray skied evening
Under shade of weary tree
Hiding from the rain
Her own wetness running like drops across leaves
And he-

Looked into her eyes with assurance; all was worthy
She-scared of promiscuity
So humbly gave into the opportunity
As wet grass blanketed her back
He atop... legs spread...
Allowing precipitation to fall in a *merengue*
Of lustful catastrophe

She was open to bleed
First time her *sangre* met his...*pene*
Yet, he marked her blood with more than lost virginity
Dropping of eternal immunodeficiency
Yet, her moans disagreed for she knew this was love
For he whispered in her ear three words
To confirm his touch. She fell-

Deeply, like the secretions releasing that she agreed
Bodies moving into darkened skies...
Deep purples and navy blues
Like the lesions that were soon to grow
Night washed out the innocence
Morning invited responsibility
Though day carried with it her lover
She was left with the memory
He was the one...Her only...H.I.V

Luvleeh Thought #13
She became what others molded her to be- broken.
-Leandrea Hill

Squalid Woman

Squalid woman
Imbruted by past lovers

Despoiled virginity
Truculent in her ways

Variegated from the beauty she once possessed
Her curly hair flowing down her back like waterfalls

Yet, knotted like a yoke

Glacial personality
Indelibly etched into her character

Superannuated---
Like stale cookies at the back of the cabinet

What caused this epochal?

The flesh that tore through her
Nine year old underdeveloped body

That left her unabashedly nihilistic---

Her Sickness

The black debri inside lungs, traveled to brain
It sat devouring the mind
So now the breath is as un-in sync as the thought

Jumping back and forth, no sense of era
Like fleas inside a carpet
Multiplying and expanding its territory
Eating whatever to survive; Acidic in nature

Bleach out the memories of good health
Smoking packs of Virginia slims
The only weight loss came from her sickness

Get this…She quit…

But cancer decided to pick up where she left off…
Helpless radioactivity fighting for victory;
All trust put in God, but life holds melancholy

Yet somehow…She always smiles…

Tobacco Burn*

Spark the lighter;
Gaseous fumes escape the purple Bic
        A small ounce of heated death
      Burns in the cigarette
  This time I'm not so Black and Mild.
  The orange glow of recession comes towards me
        Like a retreat in war and I am the enemy
Cause I choose to kill the life inside me
    Lungs blacken and throat swells,
  Yet I can't stop taking in the deadly smoke
    Truth says statistics, but it's all realistic
    Acetic Acid, found in floor wipes
Acetanisole, ingredient in perfumes
  Formaldehyde, preserves the dead
    Geraniol, found in pesticides
        Acetone, removes nail polish
    Hydrazine, found in rocket fuel
Cadmium, found in batteries
Toluene, found in dynamite and gasoline
  Cinnemaldyhyde, found in pet repellant
  Methanol, found in antifreeze
  Urea, found in pee
        Yet, I can't put down the cigarette that puts this shit in me—
          I need to subtract the addiction; And take in the oxygen— It
        ain't worth the bodily damage. The emotional toll; if I were to lose
        that one thing I love more than self -at times. The box that
        projects my craft;
        Poetry, forgive me; Body, don't leave me; I need you;
        I put out the blackened paper. Tar filled and rotting; I quit.

Fortress of Solitude

The water cascaded over my face choking
The very breath from my lungs-
Bubbles slowly counted down to zero;
...Life stood still.
I was not self.
I was that which the world tried to destroy
And I died.

I didn't try to understand the reasons
I just took in the season
Like the tide takes out the drowning
I found myself. Dead.
Yet alive in this after world

My reality is the space between time and creativity.
My art is a reflection of the dreams in my past life.
I am the misunderstood over achiever
Yet, you only see the death, for you are not a believer

Brains soaking like sponge in my head
Harsh breaths, yet, not breathing
Could I be sleeping? Drifting in my solitude
A fortress of senility;
Youth gone but trapped in my own fragility
You are lost ---

But I found my seclusion in the bottom of the sea.
Where worlds collide
I am like a zombie- neither alive nor dead
Just waiting-
        Waiting
...Wait
        ing.

Luvleeh Thought: True story

I went to a museum in Charlotte to find out some history about the New South. This Caucasian woman whose name I don't know, tapped me on the shoulder, while I was reading the information about the Ku Klux Klan. She had tears in her eyes and just grabbed and hugged me. I was feeling out of place, but I understood the moment. She apologized for all her ancestors did to mine. I humbly accepted. I told her it is up to us to create the change in society to have true equality.

That night I went home and cried. I cried for the slaves that never felt the warm embrace of their fellow white men/women-freely. I cried for the civil rights era and all those who fought for our rights. I cried for my grandfather & father who lived in the south and experienced the harshness first hand from the KKK, I cried to release the past and allow my people to start again. I wrote the following piece after the tears stopped flowing.
                                        -Leandrea Hill

Ghosts of the New South

White cape of suffrage
Daunting cloud of hope
Mockery of a people
Set out to destroy like killing a mockingbird

The clansmen of this great white nation
Like knights to a dark king
This king being oppression
Lynch out the old-Burn up the new- protection

What needs to be protected?
A belief that if you scare the masses
We won't set out for success
My blood and the blood of my people
Won't stand to be suppressed

What sheets in the night did scare?
Like ghosts haunting the countryside
Translucent to the state of existence
Wiping out a reconstruction
Through the destruction of another's being

Where a tree, green with life,
 No longer holds its beauty
Now holds marks of death, like charred wood
Its ornaments hanging from necks of common men
        Picnic in the woods- Let's celebrate
Never again, will I barbeque to that word,
Picnic, Pick-a-nigger,
        But we love traditions.

Understand what it is you're missing
Lack of knowledge, like we educate in ignorance
Take time to read, like Solomon-begin to seek
Find answers of authenticity
Inside the woods of the New South
Where their hooded ancestors
Met my dark skinned ancestors
Where we all feared change

Some say the hooded knights were scared of us
Yet we were frightened of the ghostly masks
That hid the faces of our oppressors
Terror by night- Obscurity by day
The masses gave way to the KKK.

Luvleeh Thought #14
Opening the eyes of the soul; allows for sight to all things.
-Leandrea Hill

Invisible Conversation

Conversation with a stranger gone by
Never saw him before in my life
But his presence changed the way I thought;
Mr. Jenkins the po' man sitting on the sidewalk.
Tattered clothes and broken soul/es,
Peppered beard,
Hands aged with stories from years,
Sitting on the street corner
He didn't ask for nothing
But I asked for a piece of his time.
Paid him for his wisdom
Because he didn't mind.
Sir, what causes you to be out here on the street?

It's not what you think
I had it all. I gave it up to see life from a far
The only way I knew to escape was to become invisible.

But what do you mean?
I sat and stared
I see you before my eyes...

Because you don't look through marbleized sight.
People see past what they don't want to recognize.
        So, I had to hide
Give up all I love so my flesh would die.
So I sit on this street, day out, day in and cry
People are so caught in the hype.

I used to think all that mattered was the finer things.
Women, job, clothes, hoes, shoes, games,
Drinks, clubs, cars, man... Bling was my middle name,
But money never brought the happiness.
        Just many regrets...
...I had to run, find what life was like, if I truly made it...

So, I dropped all I had and got naked,
Not in amen's and thank you Lord's —
          I don't knock how you seek
I had to connect, so I connected to the street.

Oh I see.
I understand the necessity
To un-attach the misery
From day to day
But couldn't you have chosen another way.
Now you have nothing.

You are marbleizing.
Undo the crystals,
          Stop believing the lies
And know control comes only if you allow it.
Government may say you have to bow to it
Follow laws of land and all,
But the backs of the people
Never had a choice in all their falls
So why give another dime to the cause?

I rather sit and stare and preach from my soap box
Get gawked at and spit on, but I leave people thinking
What would life be if we all were to remain invisible?
Would we see more of what matters
Or be stuck on the physical?

Mr. Jenkins-You opened my eyes.

No, you just stepped into invisible.

America- Land of the Homeless -with Da Champ*

She tried to get healthcare,
But the wealth fare line was too long
and she was hungry,
Her belly full from pregnancy
Husband without work can't provide for his family
grinding the streets daily,
Picked up fifteen dollars to eat
can't cook food, rawness- how they feed
In order to survive, struggling not to die
Living in tent in Asheville woods,
Not some broke down ghetto hood
that was the life that's good.
At least beds and warmth reside there
Not sleepless nights in the open air.
They wish for days where water could run.
Instead they wash in back alleys in basins
they cry out for help,
but Government only silences them with threats
"Lose your unborn child 'cause you're homeless"
Mother drops tears like rain drops fears
Flooding out the dirt that they sleep on
Muddy beds, same shoes…
Same threads- Listen-
this homelessness
Is the greediest poverty stricken grievance
mourning the life they had
Adorning the life that's sad
People see them and humbly turn their heads
Depression knows no aggression, voice is lost in the breeze
Couple strives for success in daily living…
No neonatal care, praying baby still breathing…
The struggle ain't happiness; only shelter, water and food
To overcome homelessness
Pieces of the puzzle to our economy
    Through forgetfulness

Take a step back and remember this...
She sits in her quiet moment of chaos
remembering the
day of August 29, 2005. Samantha the
displaced refugee
of the wrath of Neptune. He unleashed the winds
and water of death known as
Hurricane Katrina
Water falling from
watery eyes as
trees and cars flew in the sky as planes
across the lives of many.
Elderly mothers of the church praying
to their savior for the sins
of the land of voodoo and murder.
Lost in the shuffle as everything
she owns is under water. No immediate
relief for there is no
way out of this watery grave.
The buses are loaded full of
babies without milk nor medication to
save the sick.
The water flows... Stores are robbed for
any item to give a
false sense of hope that it will get better.
Sitting in the Super Dome
full of fear and prayer, Samantha is alone.
Watching suicide and
arguments for there is one bottle of water
left for a thirsty heart.
She prays... FEMA and new homes in different states
for some, deaths for
others... families are separated never
to be found. No loved ones to hug,
no cell phone
to use, Samantha my friend is
set free to Baton Rouge. After the storm to

bury loved ones and get RIP Tattoos, the people
of New Orleans begin to return,
Coming home to the aftermath to
see where she used to live. I got the
call from her voice to say
"I am safe and I found my family"
I gently cried for her. Her home and
neighborhood is now a leftover
memory that could have been mine.

As quickly as the winds blow we can be
outside the
confines of our homes. We shun
our noses at them
for the stitch. You close your windows
because they ask
for a dollar. Put yourself outside the
looking glass and
see the bigger picture. Your next sign of life
could turn into
and cardboard sign "Will work for food, God Bless You"

Homeless People are just that PEOPLE.
Treat them LIKE ONE.
Food for thought.

I Ache

I ---ache
I ache in pain suppressed behind smiles
I ache so deeply inside my womb
My children's children cry out

I ache- Knowing that I die from sickness and disease
Carried through transmissions of secretions dropping into blood streams
More than the passionate empty touch

I ache---as coughs sound like whooping winds
As blood thins like skin; Dry and shriveled
Disheveled view of life because healthcare is not at my reach
'Cause my life expectancy runs shorter than the zero's signed to your
check...

I ache--- from the neglect
That my life has a place in this corrupt world
You will never know what it feels like to have pain and be too afraid to seek
help
Because you fear the bill more than you do the results
Resting in peace seems to be the best option for many
This bill passing for health reform recreates my existence-
Relentlessly needing this change

I ache---heart beat slows down
It's never too late. Resuscitate my lungs
Get beat to regulate. It's my fate to give day to day more respect

Minute to minute
Not sure if what I feel is killing me
But I smile---as water escapes eyes
Finally seeing---hope.

I live on the edge ---
No need to have thrilling moments where my life is endanger
I live dangerously without healthcare
Caring to beat my health...before I die-
As knives carve into my sides
As pesticides seep into my cells
Tissue transforming
Organs not functioning
Pores not holding...in the fluidity of air to flesh
Soul dissects...Waiting...

For you to see value in my life
Even if I am dying-
Aren't we all?

Luvleeh Thought #15
We all fit a stereotype; but not everyone is judgmental.
-Leandrea Hill

According to Church Folks*

I--- know I been changed.
The angels in heaven done signed my name.

changed life
       "According" to the word.
found truth beyond
what preacher man says …
found culture outside
amen's, more than western Jesus
please spare me, "it's the devil"
Devilish ways brainwash people

society functions off captive thinking
media shows us the vainglorious life
of impoverished living-- church folks live in
but the devil is not in them…
only when things get put in the open.

       "According" to the gossipers
Priest fucked the church boys
Homosexuals hide in pews
First Lady Jenkins sleeping with Deacon James
All ashamed but---

I--- know I've been changed.

walk into church house
a building with more power
than the temple I live in day to day
       "According" to the church folks---
Sister Infidel married Trustee Pedophile
news is all on the board…
Ushers ushering
church folks that are too concerned
with sitting away from Malcolm
the choir director.
he better snap those hands
clap, clap, clap and dance…
 "Lord forgive me"
Sprinkle the holy oil…
…Aint that what I'm 'spose to do?

So ... I--- *know I've been changed.*

I believe in God-
not the lies that try to formulate Him
the Creator of all things
He is all in One,
collection of one Many...
church folks can't hear me
building fund collections plates
clinging too loudly---
tithe to pay Rev's car note
but church folks are funny with money

God planted in mustard seed,
faith comes
when I believe in me...
fall short He guides spiritually...

        "According" to church folks
I've died already--
Resurrected
No need for hypocrites
Find your own connections
Reincarnate living
Source power is my surge
Darkness is luminosity
Magnified optical
I am the light...

Because I--- *know I've been changed*
The angels in heaven done signed my name.

Brrrrat Tat

Brrrdat tat tat philly kat kow
Homage to the runway queen; he be she—
She got u like dayum...
Is that a man?
Answer is yes and you sit stuck
Wondering -*what the fuck?*
Never getting respect, does it still exist?
The gay man might be the straight man's wish
Or maybe not just playing the devil's advocate

Too much emphasis on sexuality,
And not mentality,
Sexual orientation
Has nothing to do with how one thinks
It reflects the sexual preference
Of what one likes to eat or drink
Jokes to ease the tension,
You know not to mention
Pastor was looking at the deacon,
But I'm letting the kat out the closet now...
Brrrdat tat tat philly kat kow

I see rainbows reflected throw diamonds,
But others want to kill
Ignorance and bands against lifestyles,
But nobody sees the shit
Going on with Heterosexuals
No, no—because God
Came down on Sodom and Gomorrah
So easy to forget
He did the same to the whore; the adulterer
All sin is weighed the same
But look —I can't call what makes him or her,
Who he or she is... sin—
I tried it...but oddly got more confused.
All it did was,

Take my sex life and place it in others views...
You might not agree
But then again who are YOU?

Judge me, but I still will stay true
I like how image sets he, she or tranny apart—
I just hate the hate crimes lashing in the air
In all walks of life people stare.
So, I admire the queen, respect the dom
Love the dyke, kiss the bi—salute the tranny
I see past your physical
I see past your sexual
I see into the person whose personality alone
Makes me analytical

So, I like hitting up the club with pride
For a great show spending dollars all night
And screaming out loud!
BRRATTDAATT TAT TAT PHILLY KAT KOW!!!

Luvleeh Thought #16
When a poet retires from poetry,
do his words no longer have meaning?
-Leandrea Hill

The Poet Called

The poet called
Said he can no longer carry on
For he has written all of which he can say
That thoughts, no longer process
In ways that stimulate his mind

Now he drifts into prose gleefully
So, why do tears stream from me?
He decides to commit suicide poetically
Which seems to be the only option
As life transforms
Poet no longer sees expression through his poetry

The legacy is written
The unity that tied
The hearts that abide
You never know a good thing 'til it's gone
These words have all new meaning

He was my confidant
...For words...
Admiring his vernacular, like a small child to parent

I listened
Though I may have seemed distant

I drew him into my thinking
Allowed his words to speak to my spirit...
And now it's those same feelings I run to as he pulls the safety...
Gun cocked and trigger ready
Taking away all of me...
Or at least what I've become....

Breaking shields allowing me to blossom
And words that slip across lips
That I didn't read ....
Took advantage of the chemistry...

Now I will miss he... the old he,
Who loved words as much as the sun loves glowing...
The one who painted pictures,
Like God created the inhabitants of this multi dimensional living
See he brought me to a deeper part of myself

Grateful
How many ways can emotion be described
I feel it's endless but in his eyes
He must slip to retirement
Something I never thought possible
He just came into my mental
To leave so soon- searching for lesson
        Within these blues
He passes torch of eternal flame

The importance of cherishing
Those whom you respect without shame
If I could get just one more day

Shots fired...
        Death awaits...
Blood seeps onto paper blending ink to red stained memories
The irony in the death of a poet

Blaq Majik

*

*Painting of an Eye by Leandrea Hill

*Poets' tongues and minds
Verbiage of ancestors;
Souls of spoken word.*

Necessity to Write

The necessity to write
Not a simple haiku
Not a sonnet or villanelle

Just the desire to get back the pen
And trust it to the paper
That my thoughts will flow with ease
Like a brush of paint sweeping greens blues and mahogany
As in the days of Michelangelo
Where a ceiling becomes the canvas to my ingenuity

I am poetry
Full of imagery
Alliteration and density
I am what you want to be
The poet in the mind of a writer
The story within the fiction and non
The creator in creativity

I steer the student
I teach the teacher
I am but a word in your memory
I am but the truth to your infidelity
For your lies have raped the innocence of mentality
Thinking on spirituality
It's more universal than psychology
A challenge for you to follow this flowing ink
I am the rhythm to your melody

Waiting in action
While you sift through last year's stanzas
I'm writing futuristic lines of your destiny.
This is just who I am...
For who I am is Luvleeh

Sequence

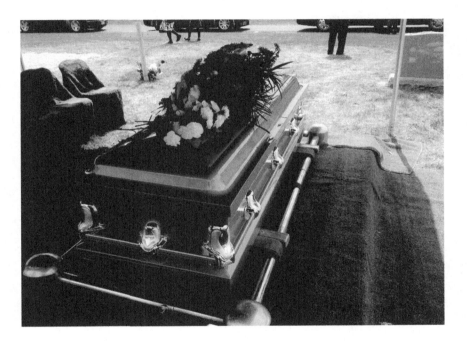

* Leandrea Hill

Money corrupts greed
Human corrupts the money
Death follows human

Luvleeh Thought #17
I'm shooting with bullets of intelligence...
-Leandrea Hill

Gun Shots

Pop, pop, pop, I shot you
Gunned down another brother
Don't care what I told you
Cause you're lost out in the gutter
Passing time high in disgust
Don't see yourself floating in the sewer
Dirt filled rat infested ghetto
But it's what you rep, 'cause you can't let go
Afraid of achievement beyond the projects
What projection you don't get is education
Build a future beyond disgrace and
Get off the lyrics of a fake life gangster
So achievement won't be cell block loser
0-1-8-A dash 0-2-1-Fakester
Yet you party like a rock star, selling the rock star
White, green, black lone star; Rep'ing colors like rainbows, yet
You call me gay---

Pop, pop, pop, I shot you
Baby pushing baby in carriage I got you
Not like in the past when a doll is what you practiced on
Now it's the real thing and the father's gone
Not all cases have a happy song
You singing out the same old sad song
Hollering I'm grown,
Still on curfew cause you're in your mama's home
Similac, welfare and your daddy's gone,
Blaming it on him, cause he left you alone
Poor excuses from ghetto dimes cause the money's wrong
Count your pennies towards a better cause,
Step up your pride and live strong
No need to continue a cycle of dependence on---
"Baby, don't leave-who's she? And I thought we had more"
Should have told you, he thought you were a whore.
One man too many, now your friend's out the door

You standing there as a joke with a crying baby in one arm
Let it go. It can't cause you more harm,
Embrace your life and live hard
For you were God's gift when you were born---

Pop, pop, pop, I shot you
Stop blaming society for your troubles and check the source
Got a system run off ignorance
Where our babies make more sense
Country shot up with bullets of blindness
Got it so bad mother-nature trying to destroy us
Yet a Pres. must be dense
To not be present in this awakening
No longer sleeping on the belief that there is unity
For I can't recall the last time I had coffee with Susie
Nor she with me; What is unity defined?
When I can't get how a population of my people
Don't exist in my society, rather a gated community.
Funny, some things we do have in common---

Pop, pop, pop, I shot you
Domestic violence hitting up crimes
Worse than your forefather's hangings
Why do we have to keep on destroying?
Can't find safety in our homes
Cause the streets some days feel safer
Cause the gunshots make their rounds clearer
As you get closer to the fighters
'Til you see who holds the trigger
Small hand, Small faces, sh- its someone's little brother
All works together cause black on black
Done spread to black on other
No care in the world, they'll shoot your mother
What can we do to solve this mass murder?
Slaughtering each other like Iraqi war soldiers---

Pop, pop, pop, I shot you

Got more military men and women dying
For a war we don't know the cause of.
One man can't even speak right
But we defend his thoughts towards foreigners
Money being spent so fast for problems we create
But the streets here are full of people who can't make it
The dumb sh- celeb's do is lame
Like adopting kids from Africa
When the agencies here are overflowing so fast
The kids choose to remain, unnoticed never claimed
And you wonder why they go insane
It's a cycle that needs to end.
See how one man who fails to succeed
Can make the youngest person fail to achieve
Damn this country-
If it's going to allow this hell to up rise any longer
I strapped up ready to fight back
Reclaim my children, my people and future---
Bullets flying out of intelligence---
Pop, pop, pop, I shot you.

Blind Theories*

I don't understand
Why there is so much confusion in this world
Where everyone thinks they have the answer to everything
Everyone pointing at what the next person is doing
Wrong, but fail to see they are standing in the mirror.
Folks earning Ph D's; People hating Deliberately

What's with the hatred and publicity
News casting all the chaos that positivity is the new disease
People spreading their thoughts like venomous injections
Yet what is the solution?
Resolutions of militants like endless wars
Why are we acting like past presidents...
Obama not moving fast enough,
So folks are second guessing
Having another reason to create more oppression

The ratio of unemployment is still rising,
While jobs are going overseas
Or to prison systems that enslave the broken society
Why do young men and women continue the cycle
To be locked in security?
What is secure in this ... you can't control anything
Incarcerated dreams; didn't think it would be dollar a day jobs And
chain gangs
Without a chance because someone is waiting
With a bullet and your name's on it

Shame on it--- cause drugs run thought process
'cause thugs run street progress
And those who are not exposed, luck becomes the draw
As they turn and forget those who don't have more

I was lucky—my parents broke down the necessity
To strive beyond the certainty

That man can only gain what he believes
So if that is the case
Then why the fuck am I still in this community…
Struggling with the best of them for a voice
Beyond the paper, Legislators ignoring the violence
It's insane!
Why are kids killing kids like games?
Like we are the P.S.P; Poverty Seeking Poverty
Spend your money to make the 1% richer
Can't pay rent but your clothes are dapper
It's a shame you had to die for your shoes
Pasts haunting you like past paradigm ghosts
What does it cost in your conscious?
While you're stuck in subliminal
The subconscious is a default
You need to rearrange the settings
Get it broadcasting
The changes you need to take to make a living
Stop this recession thinking
You had nothing before the gov't started losing
So you should know how to step above the confusing
Media hype blasting stories about us like we are the savages
Yet corporate stay confessing
Sleeping with whores and prostituting
Like they do our nation
They forget those who made them
See ancestors built the bricks they burn
In night caps of infidelity, Adultery
Whatever you think will get your rocks off and not get seen
Like we don't live in a world of TV, Tell –advise the scandals
Stop acting like you can't handle this truth---

Luvleeh Thought #18
We, the people, are the only beasts of this world.
-Leandrea Hill

The Hunted

Steps out the door to broken cement sidewalk
Brick building project holding up the block
No grass in parks; Nor kids
Slanging guns in backs of pants...
Loud music thumping to the rhythm of a hustler's step
Junkie feigning to get those street diamonds
Willing to work hard, $2 dollars a pop-
They gotta have that rock
It's 5:37 am and he's on the clock
Dodged bullets that rang out across the way
His boy got hit with a stray
This is the street jungle where they stay
People hunted liked animals
Targeted for those cannibals
Eating them alive before they have a chance to live
Only 19 years old, but lost his soul
Missed two court dates; they charge him
Left behind bars unable to move
Had four months 'til graduation
Prisoner of actions took
Decisions that made him victim to the box

~Third Blossom: The Stories Untold~

The Stories Untold: *The beauty of life is the relationships it creates. I always enjoy the process of creating new friendships, relationships or building with family. Although sometimes these relationships may altar; you move on, people part through death or a change of heart; each experience still holds a lesson. It is these lessons that draw us closer to knowing who we are as people.*

Sometimes it takes the worse in others to see the best in ourselves... We learn that everything we allow ourselves to endure is in the power of our hearts and minds. Knowing when to let go; or whether to take a chance is important.

Sometimes we have to rely on others and our experience is out of our control. I.e.- Loved ones in military, youth obeying parents, breakups or loss of a loved one etc, but I've learned to embrace these moments for the lesson will come along with time.

I am blessed to have family and friends who have endless memories to share with me throughout my life. We have been through some wondrous experiences, although some were well... let's just say ... they were not as exciting. Nevertheless, I cherish the joys of all life experiences; good and bad. This blossom reflects the moments on "good & bad" days, people and relationships.

Luvleeh Thought #19
Your voice cues into my ear,
like a sweet humming bird in the morn.
-Leandrea Hill

Take Me There with Brandon McCoy*

Briefly He Pauses
Fists nestled Boldly
Above his hips...
Gazing over his left shoulder,
He smiles
Looking back at her
Triumphantly he stands
Giving her one last look at black Adonis
Before he vacates
Leaving her slumped in the doorway
Dazed...
Apparent, as her bottom lip
Still quivers...
Aftershock of his lingering touch
The doorframe provides assistance
As her legs are the same consistency as mashed potatoes
...still being creamed
Her mind is racing,
He's her track star muscles and all
Validated by midnight exams of endurance...
She's barely able to close the door
As she remembers...
The large, strong hands
That squeezed her supple behind
Providing leverage...
... to be effortlessly lifted
Knees instinctively part
Unlocking a natural aphrodisiac
Immediately temperature rises
As bodies press against each other
Lips lock in passion
Attempting to communicate nonverbally
Begging each other to
"Take Me There"

Where unspoken words
Are engraved in circles
Along napes, bosom, thighs

Where eyes lock in the sunlight
Tracing journeys of black horizons
Stipule passion
Growing into African violet
Multiple respirations

Contrarily as two
Begin to find 69 ways
To make the Earth –quake

Amatory embrace~~~
Lover's scouring debris
Of internal walls
Fallen from aftershock
While thrusting winds carry her moans
Like music against airwaves

She's lyrics against his tongue
Words lick up every drip of her ink...
Swilling the flavor of written words
Like banned books... a forbidden love

Hands lost in ogees...
Enticed bodies
That climatically swallows rain

Savage wet hair...
Against back...
He inhales her aroma...

Warming his soul...
Lively and bubbly
As sun dippin' into the ocean

Studying her abyssal plain
He- marine biologist
She- his bioluminescence

Overcome by her quintessence
Electromagnetic waves---
He increases amplitude
Against her polarization
Magnificence ---

Third Eyes gazing while lost in epidermis
Laying in the mist of stares
Simultaneously knowing...
Each was taken "there".

Luvleeh Thought #20
To know your true worth is to count the jewels in your
life.
-Leandrea Hill

Gem In Eye *

She is that which you desire
Her mind is intrinsic
         You see the curl of her hair
I see the d.n.a that wraps thoughts of knowledge
Passed down from generation to generation
She is Goddess, Queen of her essence
The reflection of God is within her
Who knows beauty, not physical alone
But eyes, can only tell you her story
She knows how to direct her path
         You see the wood beneath her canvas

I see the blocks she's overcome.
Lying down; Mysterious glare
         You want to feel like her back---What it is she bears?
Her poetry speaks; Her silence speaks
Gem in Eye are jaded but not poetically
Yet calls herself the Jaded Poet
Weary of those who take for granted her gifts
She speaks to the world but like a breeze you may miss
She is in limbo of your acknowledgement
Her lips part; Her thoughts escape
I hear--- I wait; I draw in her experience
As though it is my own, a song bird in the chaos of ignorance
Knowledge is not bliss, it is encouragement
That wisdom is not lost
         She is . . . that which some fear
But others choose to emulate
         She is . . . in my existence,
My atmosphere joins to hers universally through verse
Yes, I feel what others concur
She is the stanza
         I am the word
Together we are poetry
She is Poetically Free
Her eyes just tell the story.

Γψπσιε Δοῶε (Gypsy Dove)*

Beautiful winged dove
White feathers ruffled
No longer live in cage
Reflections of tethered past
Wings can now spread for stage

It being sky, the sun a guide
Nature-- called back to revive
Survival no longer for fit
The wind –A friend
A lover - Who is like God~
Overcome fears of being overtaken

The seasons continuously change
Gypsies belly dance in the rain
All around this dove with clover in its mouth
Its song vibrating the melody
Tap, tap, tap- the tambourine
Step, step, step- she's serene

Beautiful gypsy dove
I sing to you, I honor you
Like auburn gold and tangerine
Marinate the leaves
The admiration of natural riches
Rebirth in this beauty
Each year a new
Each year freer than before
Searching, finding, being Adour

Luvleeh Thought #21
Father's love their children; though sometimes not
understood- growth comes with age.
- Leandrea Hill

Daddy I Never Said

Daddy, I never said how much I love you
For making the monsters go away from beneath my bed.
That what scared me about the sheets was what the covers held
Inside
The night mares from molested youth
How hands found ways into places I didn't know could be
Abused
On the physical, yet leave scars on emotional
Only to have me doubt the spiritual, since my soul
Had long sense abandoned me, like the protection I thought I
Needed
Told to keep secret-but; Daddy, it's ok you didn't know.
For so long I was too afraid to tell you because you
Beat the fear into me at such an innocent time
Afraid
To let you know your niece would manipulate my mind
Telling stories too mature for my imagination
Only to allow her hands to explore my
Creation
Daddy… I wanted your protection.
I understood too much before my time,
but I never said how much
I love you,
That I don't blame you …anymore.
I don't blame you for… what you couldn't control,
I just wish the way you would come at me for the miniscule
You could have done to my molester, take her and beat her
For doing SEVEN years of storytelling.
The "devil" used my gift against me…
Made it so hard to step into my destiny
But Daddy---
I wrote this to say I love you
I can't let what either of us didn't know
Continue to tear at my mental, physical…or emotional
Because you are not the same man nor I girl
I remember the long nights…working providing and being
Father…

I know you did your best to protect and love,
Even if my memories want to fade the truths
I know I was always your

Little Girl...
I just had to release this pain soaked into my tissue
No matter what... I must reunite soul with spiritual
So please know I forgive you as much as I know is possible
You Loved Me...
So for that... water absorbs into my cheeks
I love you daddy- though I never may have said.

Luvleeh Thought #22
The stories of the broken cry out louder in silence;
Listen to the wind- it speaks their truth.
-Leandrea Hill

Unheard Diary

He needed to free
So when he parted her legs
Like her lips around his piece
She told him to stop
This was not how she wanted it to be
She was told about candles- music and chemistry
Yet the only music was the rocking of the washing machine
To muffle her soon to be screams

He told her to get on the floor
Where piles of clothes bore comfort to cold wood planks
Darkness taking shape
She closed her eyes in order to visualize
What she didn't have. This was not new-
Though her first voluntarily---
She bit her lip and he carried in his army...
Stroking away what she held as virginity

Grateful for 100 proof Vodka that numbed her pain...
Blood trickles the strain of orgasm
Contracting more than the rise and fall of her walls
He was inside her---

But she was inside the prison---
Or nightmares replaying in her bosom
As he bit at her breasts---
Squeezing the last bit of breath

As hands grabbed neck to hush---
Complying for fear of fighting back
Would end her plea for help...
So she took it like any woman would; Right?
She knew her place that night...

He grinned at her weezing...
Thought he was the man pleasing
Dropping off his seeds with invasion
A war broke out in her womb

Now two months later finds child conceived through rape
Std's just guaranteed her fate...
Wanting more of love she didn't abort
Needing child to give her more

Of what her parents never had...
Lustfully unborn --- she wrapped her arms around belly
Singing lullaby's of heart break...
She turned to pimp the one who created her namesake

For she had nowhere else to turn
But tricks kept her flowing
Not knowing how hard it would be to run
So she shakes her ass and cums- with baby inside---
Can't judge for she knows wrong as her right

At seven months she prematurely gives birth---
To 2 lb infant ---smaller than her pride
She wanted to die that night...
Induced by the overdose of crack...
She long since turned to on streets that lacked
Her needs---

So--- baby girl was born to the prostitute,
Crack addicted teen
Forced that way cause her value was never weighed
She should have stayed the unnamed victim
Instead she's someone's mother
Staged for lesson...

Won't hear about her in your newspaper
Until she makes the first page
Slain... Baby Found In Bag---
Mother with a bullet through her brain.
Street dreams;
The unheard diaries.

Hush Little Baby *

> *Hush little baby, don't say a word*
> *Momma's gonna buy you a mocking bird...*

Babies weep in the arms of their mother,
Little mind not knowing what is wrong
Only seeing change in situations.
Pink becomes a dark shade of red;
The bruises ---hitting faces
Small hands reaching out
Crawling from the darkness to try and hide;

> *Hush little baby, don't say a word...*

The babies need protection
Trusting that which is supposed to love them
Hurt by the ones that curse them
Victims to the hand that destroys them
Never seeing past the moons of childhood;
Never knowing the difference between right and wrong
Their playgrounds become empty with despair.
Voices cry out but are muted- pain instated
Hurt babies- left in the wooded

> *Hush little baby, don't say a word...*

Toys have turned sodden
Rotten like the souls of their destroyer
Let them suffer while the babies are in the arms of the creator
Recreating; explaining why they never got to fulfill a long life
Could it be--- that so many babies never see the light of day past three
Four or five--- youth die at the hands of the adults in misery
Close your eyes---dream of fairytales and mystical stories

Hush little baby don't say a word
Momma's gonna buy you a mocking bird
But if that mocking bird don't sing---
My heart loves you ---in eternal---sleep...

Don't Drop the Eggs

Two brown beauties
Too young to know life's challenges
Walk the gravel road to the town grocer
Singing simple lullabies and skipping here and there
As they collect lilies and dandelions along the path
Surrounded by tall corn stalks
And hidden bugs....that hummed along with them
In their travels

The sun crackled against the dry land...
Heat raising in the distance along the way...the girls
Barefoot on this road; like walking on coals
Yet, still enjoyed the occasional breeze
List in hand of eldest child
"Mommy says, don't drop the eggs, they are fragile"

The two reach town and gather what is needed
Not noticing eyes that wander
Lips that lick in the smoldering humidity
As weed dangles at his mouth's corner
Straw hat bent to block the glare...as he stares...

The girls are anxious to get home
From their first visit to the store alone
"Careful don't drop the eggs, they're fragile"
All the while... the sun reaches its highest peak
Feet continue to beat against stone...

Snap...the woods talk back...
Torn bags ...small muted cries...
Brown eyes spill red tears...
As the eggs lay shattered on the drain rocks...
Bubbling...next to chewed weed
All that is left on a Saturday morning
Small fingers clasped into interlocking hands...
Still...
As a mockingbird sings a poignant lullaby...

Polka Dots and Stripes

Whooping stick flogs
Whipping through
Air, the sound of sliced wood
She feels its sting

Black eyes like polka dots along her tattered skin
The stripes of her refuge

She succumbs from his blows
But yet she doesn't let go
Holding onto the limbs of love

Broken torso, limp over the branches
Leaves only crimson with affirmation
Wilted destroyed in this cycle
No solidity in this treason

Betrayal of a season
Screams cry out with pleas
Yet nothing is heard over the whacking
Hacking at a soul with disparity

Burning like flames
Against this woman
She has not given up
Her polka dots compliment her stripes
But her life is no longer
A work of art.

The breath parts.
The leaves fall.
The last blow strikes.

Once Upon A Time

She let him in...
Saying "I don't mind sharing this place I call home"
He was without
when she had all she needed-
family pleaded...
But the not's that knotted-tied in her wants
She ignored her sixth sense

That told her he can't be trusted
Thrust-him into a deal...
Where heart chose to feel
So she said yes come live with me for a while
Inviting her demons to live freely in her domain
it was a claim to her glory
that her story would remain
Unknown to those around her
although sadly it still haunts her in her dreams
As daylight only protects her thoughts
for in darkness lies her memories
Cries shrieked out
Please don't hurt me I'll do anything
Just don't take away my prized entities
But words fell on deaf ears as she muffled screams
so they would not fall into her children's fears
Mommy --- holding in all she had
to give herself as sacrifice for this
Thief---
Who boldly invaded her womb
Tearing limb from soul
Slowly as it bled
her pierced wound
he took of her flesh
gnawing like savage beast..
this demon... was he
eyes glazed; staring

she could no longer fight
forced her to settle in and take it
so she did
if only it meant the minutes would become seconds until it
was over
when self pride and humility;
were left to the dogs---
how many times God must she suffer as this vessel
who was molested incest infected,
sold, beat and neglected,
broken and disrespected
do you not see the pattern
a cycle which should not be accepted---
but too often rejected
because when women speak out
they are to blame
so there is no shame when she holds in all she can
for the sake of her children
for the sake of society pointing fingers
for the sake of people saying it was her decision
but it wasn't

he decided to take his stroke
and strike more than her vaginal walls
he fucked her raw
like society does her daily
for being a woman scorned

But I see in her -strength; although she is torn
For she speaks out to others
Through actions not covered
She gives back
Even when nothing will replenish those horrific scars that
mark her past...
Except the love she has
Never giving up on it
As healing seeps through her veins
She acknowledges that old pain

But embraces change
As she stands above all who chose to remain
Unfaithful to a Queen
A black diamond, a white pearl, a lotus, a woman
Who despite her odds with fate
Knows her destiny is greater than her rape

I'm just taking time to tell you her story.

Luvleeh Thought #23
In this state of mind. Set me--- free.
-Leandrea Hill

Better Hope Today

Her screaming cries whaling
into the echoing mind of my existence.
For ten months I've heard this scream
and it gets louder daily

See as smiles cascade faces,
we suppress the nightmares we live in nightly
When doors close to the silence outside our hinges...
And she sits on a bed...
Leg propped in any position but comfortable and she cries

She cries...
She lies...
and says she's ok to muffle my reaction
But I know
She's hurting...
Diabetes taking toll on her body

Why didn't I try to give of myself before?
Why now do I see her worth?
Why now when pain seems to trigger her fears
Like gun shots into the air
Hitting aimlessly any target that crosses its path
She tries to laugh...

But laughter just prolongs the streaming flood
That pours down her soft blushing cheeks...
That once was my cheek to cheek softness,
Now drowns each other in moistened
I'm sorry's. But no blame...
She still remains calm in the eyes of the outsiders
Singing out all she can
Through high pitched

Lord help me's and I can't take it's
Lord's Prayer sounds like repeating songs on the radio
And there's nothing I can do...and it hurts...

Punctured wound in foot...
Pain in side, body fighting effects of age
She is the same one who did anything for anybody
Why does she suffer?

Why...

I cannot linger in this heartache
I must smile in spite of all things
For joy keeps us when we can't keep ourselves
I understand her happiness while she heals...

So I must not wade in her sorrow
There is better hope today...
I will not wait for tomorrow

Love pours out as healing energy
Once it was me she tended to every need
Now it's I...Realizing...My mom needs me.

Sailor Returns Home

A late night call short in its length
But filled with an eon of love
Simple words exchanged
"I'm home"

A mother's son returns from the brutal
contours of a Japanese shore
As he drops anchor in sky onto airline strip
The winds so gently cool the heat off a rapid heart
"I'm home"

As younger sister grabs grey cordless phone to confirm
what she already knew in her soul
"We love you-Did you do your Thank you God dance?"
As feet jump towards darkened skies
that carry more light in a single star in this moment---
as it flickers against his medals of honor-
"Yes- the whole time on the plane."

And lives are no longer the same
As family draws closer to the joys that were once so plain-
Life – the value increased again
Simple words take on stronger meaning…
 "I'm home"

Mother's praying tears reassured in the faith
She gives to her loyal God "My son is home"
She waited for one thousand ninety five days
And counts the 365 sun rises left before
Total release and his service no longer needs his active duty

When she can sleep
Through nights without tears curving her cheeks…
So she savors this call at 11:18 pm on June 1, 2010
When her son called home-

Father

It took a king to teach me what it means to know a father
One who is strong, yet still a provider
He took responsibility for the life he brought in this world
Not with one but with two precious girls

He relearned what love was in order to share it freely
He gave up the lifestyle to be in tune with his babies…
Knowing *she* would not be there to help raise
For *she* was not as strong as *she* could be

He redirected the course like Navy
Took captive his heart's loves and carried
Joy through pain –wiping tears and providing smiles…
Daddies little girls are his jewels – all the while

This was what being a father truly means….
This was what fatherhood should be…
Knowing he has seen every achievement
From first words to first honors…
To laugh at the small things and protect when in danger

He is a loyal - loving-Father…
One day he'll find his reflection
'Til then continue to grow and love harder…
Knowing love formulates a connection

His girls are his essence…
In them I see the bliss
Of a father's love---
His foundation…

Warm Innocence of Spring[*]

Children's feet beating on the soft green grass

The breeze blows in from my window
While the sun caresses my face as I watch

Innocently, they roam the yard playing
Once before, that was me

The first dance after the earth wakes from its sleep
Laughter singing its praises through the streets

While the grill barbeques,
The honey soaked chicken and pigs feet

I keep my head high,
As I nurture the child within my body

She Speaks

Consuelo D. Hill circa 1973

She spoke to me in-
Simple breezes through ruffled
Pine; She spoke to me…

Luvleeh Thought #24
Take the night in a lustful dance of two spirits
intermingling upon the dance floor of flesh.
-Leandrea Hill

Undeniable Lust *

Linking to your hook, I feel a tug at my imagination
You got me reeled into your orgasmic creation

I do not want to be released
Take me into captivity
Where I can be your nourishment for living
Become a part of your growth and being

I don't need the ring to bring forth thanksgiving
You and I intersect, so that alone is freeing

Let me wake to your touch; where dreams escape
Find you canvassing my landscape
In search of the rose that hides in the bush
Trimming my hedges with a gentle brush

Confirmation my garden is not forbidden
I open for penetration

You forgetting she and I forgetting he
We will simply be an immoral melody
Play the chords to our disloyalty
I need to be the keeper of your *DNA*---please,

Come out with truths and become my reality
I cannot *conceive anything less than being your queen*
Within *my walls*-deeply,
Is the path to prosperity
Dancing in the morning dew; I feel you –
Deep penetrating in my soul

Self departing spiritual, I am in your control
Releasing to this moment of rendezvous
Yes, lust is lovable
But to love this lust is undeniable.

Echoes Against A Brick Wall*

Jamala Milele Lott, http://confessionsofa.webs.com/confessions.htm

*Naturally flawless
Smooth black skin echoes her curves
Singing across brick*

Voice of My Pussy

I-stay on-the-tip of his tongue
Like honey dipped and tasteful
I am the reason why his sweet tooth never yearns for attention
I am his pleasure candy...
We go at it in any hour; any day; any place
'Cause he likes it nasty

Legs creamy smooth caress his cheeks
As he runs his face down to my pillow soft thighs
He dives into his dreams head first and wanting
Never to wake, as my body shakes
And responds to his subconscious...

Knocks me unconscious ...but for a moment
He took over my mind... through my pussy
Reaching inside my thoughts
One then two fingers guiding his tongue's stroke

Water flowing as he's rowing... down my Nile
Lips open and inviting... Cervix ready to receive
All he has to give me... Lips lick to a puckered kiss
Tongue trailing down breasts,
As hands shift legs like Tectonic plates
And his anaconda finds its way into my river

Body shivers... Names scream out in bliss
He knows each turn through my cliffs
Walls giving way to his dick
He's got that Oh shit!- sex... Making our own flicks
Take me, flip me, smack it
Make thighs respect it
Cause sweat drips to fall down- as we -slow grind in hips

Hair wild and muscles contracting
His arms flexing... Abs tense through in and out
Lift and release; squirting my response to he
And him searching me; Deeply...
I stay on-the-tip of his tongue
Can't you see when he tastes me?
He takes in all of my magic
I am medicine to his orgasmic

All he has to do is lick suck and live
My womb gives him everlasting life
I am his ... all knowing thoughts
His ... heart mind and soul
His ...first and last words
Cause... I stay on the tip of his tongue

So when he speaks my pussy is heard
Listen to what he says, vocalizing passionate obsessions
I love it when he speaks my language
Off-the-tip of his tongue

Luvleeh Thought #25
Everyone desires an ultimate orgasm in everything they
do; sex is just the one thing we relate it to.
Don't be so shy to let out your inner orgasms (joys)
wherever you are--- you'll be surprised at how they create
a better experience through each part of your journey.
-Leandrea Hill

Painted Thoughts

I painted his face in order to capture what imaginary can be...
So when he comes I know I will have drew him to me
That my energy sent out an S.O.S to save me from insecurities
That one day I will find my Mr. Ooh Wee
Bite my lip, wink my eye & feel chemistry

This man will drift out the canvas of my mind
Allowing our colors to intertwine
Through walks in parks and conversations over candle lights
Not about what I have between my thighs

Unlock tombs within the pyramid of our encounter
My heart be stolen like thieves in the narrow corridors
Escape the traps to put me on display in a museum
Have my hieroglyphics painted on his heart and;

He will learn my history
Give into me~ Like Hyperboles
He will taste my thoughts and write out my recipe
For I love passionately
He will sense this when I kiss his cheek gently
Never moving too fast~ I'm a lady...

My curves will glide toward him as we stroll
Telling all he needs to know...
But knowing all the answers already
For my image compliments his photography
Capturing the moment in hues of mahogany

Photogenic genetics
That carbon copy our future aesthetics
He causes my heart to pound at rates
Surpassing repetition...
It beats as one sound mimicking his syncopation

Ripples of his brown skin leave me salivating...
Let me drink of his water to purify me
Images become thoughts as the horizon, jealous of his rooted beauty,
Manipulates the sun to hide...
Leaving his silhouette to engulf my mind
Let me be his lips, so his tongue can lick
My sweetness, after candy coated kiss
He's got me in a twist

My words coming out backwards
? bliss my be you can; Flip it
Can you be my bliss?
I like him sensually melodic...

I painted him to be rhythmic to my consciousness
Never met in physical but I feel him in my spirit.
He is blessed for two angels kissed his cheeks–
Dimples signify his heavenly–
Connection–
Smile draws in my affection
No rejection;
Submission, I give myself to him...
Although, he's just an image on my canvas.

Her Eyes

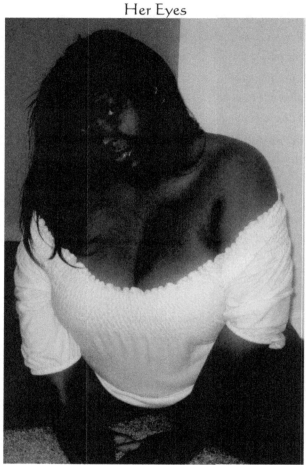

My Sister Jeneta Tunnell

She gives you her heart;
Open to take in your love;
Mind lost in her eyes.

Without A Word

Music speaks for me
Body language replies
          Close our eyes
Lightly caress cheeks memorizing each curve
Open-gaze into eternity

          Sit back-to-back
Deeply inhale and exhale
Feel our heartbeats through backbones
          Face forward...
Thrill me with butterfly kisses
After soft kiss to forehead;
          Hold my face in your hands,

Slightly open your mouth when done
Only to trace our lips with tongues-
          Explore new kissing spots
Nibble along the nape of your neck
Kiss the tips of your fingers
The back of your knees

          Lying closely; massaging
Small of my back... drop Godiva kisses tenderly
As you submerge into my side
          Tickling... with your nose

Place my arms around your neck
Re-live the first moment of falling in love
Nerve endings delicately sensitive to your charge
          Ionic release, feeling atomic inside

Your chest expands only as mine
Retracts; just long enough
For my breath to cool
Your countenance

Blinking slows
Eyes close letting hands talk
Again...Oceanic waves part the pink sea
Leaving ship wrecked
Us; two survivors
Clinging for the last bit of love...
Every time as if our last...
Yes... *"You got me...speechless"*

Sun Kissed*

*Barron Davis & Leandrea Hill

The sun saw our love
And built a dream on our kiss
Each time passion shines

Apologies

Forgiveness;
the last phase of healing before you move forward

He ended it
...She agreed
Both were not in a place to share energy
The mirror
no longer reflected
their image as one
It blurred;
as though a steamy hot shower never ended
over their relationship
Washing with it their love.

So, friends left as lovers;
wanting more in passionate embrace from the other

She called
...And got his voicemail
He texted
...And she erased it
They crossed paths at the grocery store
...But neither spoke;
It was too late...

Sleepless nights beating on their hearts and minds
Thoughts of why did she let his love go?
Months passed,

She walked down the brick of the boardwalk
Looking to the distance of the peer...
There he stood...
In their old spot...
watching the same sun set into the fiery ocean
Wind blowing into her ear...*go*

She reached out and touched
His shoulder;
He turned and caught
Her shadow across the dock
180 degrees confirmed the figure;
He reached his arms out
She fell into his grasp
...Lips lost themselves
in a familiar kiss
Seagulls watched from the railing...
Sun winked against the water's edge
...fading...
As their break up
Sealed itself in love once again...

Talking into the night...
The earth wrapped them
in laughter and I missed you's
Hands clasped in a firm bond.

He forgave her; she accepted his apologies;
Both not blaming other,
For strengthening the other to live more...
Each confirmed
that universe brought them back together
This time...
honesty, openness, unity embraced them as one...

Love took over...
Lust subsided to a seductive passion
Filled with truth...
Yes,
... comes to the light...everything.

~Sakura Thoughts~

This section is for you to write your own thoughts about love, life and relationships- Sakura: A Luvleeh Experience-of your own.

Tell yourself; How can you find your own blossoms? Plant your Sakura Thoughts here. Take the time to recognize your growth- by loving yourself truly from the heart; watering your seed; and recognizing the stories untold. These are things to uplift you daily.

Every day is a new experience. Place the desires of the heart here. Those you wish to experience in the next 6 months, 1 year, and 5 years. I know 5 years ago I desired to be an author and I'm here now.

6mo:

_____
_____
_____
_____
_____
_____
_____
_____
_____
_____
_____
_____
_____
_____

1yr:

_____
_____
_____
_____
_____
_____
_____
_____
_____
_____
_____
_____
_____
_____
_____
_____
_____
_____

5yrs:

What is your favorite poem and why? How did it affect you? Write this here and send me a copy to luvinksnlinks@gmail.com. I thank you ahead of time for reaching out.

Finally, if you can take the time each day to wake up and create your bliss in order to create your greatness would you? Then 1 encourage you to begin today. Live your dreams by stating positive affirmations to achieve your above goals. Taking the first step today; means you are heading in the right direction for a better tomorrow. Below place a mantra (positive affirmation) that will encourage you to become a greater person daily. Read it daily whenever you need to morning, midday, after school, before work, at night, when things are good and when they aren't so good. 1 promise you'll find yourself becoming more encouraged to do and be better.

Have fun with this!

_____
_____
_____
_____
_____
_____
_____
_____
_____
_____
_____
_____
_____
_____
_____
_____
_____
_____
_____
_____
_____
_____
_____
_____
_____
_____
_____
_____
_____
_____

~Who is Luvleeh Poetiklocks?*~

Leandrea "Luvleeh Poetiklocks" Hill is an artist who paints pictures with her words. She is a poet born to write. There are many layers of Leandrea Hill which create the poet, artist mentor, volunteer and entrepreneur known as *Luvleeh Poetiklocks*.

She graduated from Elizabeth City State University in 2006.Relocated to Charlotte, NC, where she was a substitute teacher, "Girlfriends" Mentor; showcased "Love, Life & Relationships, a one woman poetry show at the Golden Arrow Plaza in VA; was V.P. of non-profit organization, Youth H.O.P.E. International under founder ***Vinroy Reid***; & featured at various locations prior to relocating back to NY, 2009.

In NY, she launched her writing/ performance career and small business. Currently, author of two books of poetry; *Sakura: A Luvleeh Experience Volumes 1 & 2*, (Volume 2 release date TBA). Author of "L.I.P.S: A Collection of Poems" (2011) and "Strokes of a Petal's Edge: The Chapbook" (2011); two self published limited edition chapbooks. She has performed for "I M A Poet", SleuthProPresents "Lyrics", The Culinary Institute of America & various other programs/ venues supporting the arts in the NY area. She is the Host for "Newburgh's Open Mic" of Newburgh, NY at The Wherehouse. She is the creator of *Unity Through Poetry* and *Spreading Unity Through Poetry* in which she facilitates an online forum and offline events. "Luvleeh" spreads UTP in all aspects of her life. She continuously gives back to others by networking with people willing and desiring to spread Unity Through Poetry. She hosts "Verbal Illustrations": *the workshop* for youth aged 5-18 and *the open mic* for youth and community. She also facilitates a poetry workshop for women called "Finding Your Voice".

Leandrea's small business, *Luvleeh Inks & Links;* handmade jewelry, arts, crafts & poetry, is where she distributes all forms of her works to the public. Her brand states, "To be unique is to be Luvleeh and to be Luvleeh is to be one of a kind." Through her business, she has volunteered and donated gifts, poetry and time to her surrounding community.

Her favorite quotes:

"Wisdom is the river between reality and imagination. Don't let ignorance flood your waters."
                              - Leandrea Hill

"Love begets Love, Unity begets Unity, Peace begets Peace, which all together begets *Unity through Poetry*"
                   - Luvleeh Poetiklocks, Huniie & Indigo

Feel free to contact Leandrea "Luvleeh Poetiklocks" Hill at the following:

Email: luvinksnlinks@gmail.com
FB Group Pages: "Spreading Unity Through Poetry" OR "Newburgh's Open Mic"
FB Product Page: "Luvleeh Inks & Links"
Twitter: @LuvInksNLinks
Blog: "Poetik Rendezvous" luvleeh.wordpress.com
Youtube Channel: poetiklocks
Website: www.wix.com/LuvleehPoetiklocks/Luvleeh
Other sources: unitythroughpoetry.wordpress.com
                          phoenixstar9online.com

Stay tuned for the sequel:
"Sakura: A Luvleeh Experience Volume 2"

~Appendix~

Acknowledgements

Unity Through Poetry- is a mantra I stated often that has since become a movement. It encourages the support of your fellow artists/artists communities. This includes new book & album sales, links to help writing, overall well–being of artists & supporters as well as supports both live or online based events for the arts. There is a Facebook group page called "Spreading Unity Through Poetry" which I started during this writing journey. Here, we truly connect the artists and it is open to all forms of the arts. We believe: "Love begets love; Unity begets Unity; Peace begets Peace; which all together begets Unity through Poetry."- Luvleeh P.(me), Huniie, Indigo

First Blossom: A Heart of Hearts

Photo of Sakura Painting- Photographer *Leandrea Hill*,

"Winter" Photo -My friend, *Poet Barron Davis* founder of "Ra-poetry (Rap-paah-tree)" & I winter 2010 at a venue for Luvleeh Inks & Links. www.wix.com/barrontdavis/raven

"Love's Requisition" *Poet K. Martai Richardson-* A poet, a veteran & great friend, who has published his first book of poetry *Reflections of a Man's Soul*, found on www.martaipoetry.com. This poet opens up his soul in each of his writes; exposing the reader to the artist within.

"Love's Requisition"- italicized words are from India Arie's "Ready For Love" words are sung during live performance. This song was more of an inspiration behind the write.

"Portal to My Soul" Photo - These eyes are yours truly. Taken Fall of 2009. During this time, I began a soul search that I am still continuing to grow on. It's a great place to be.

"Knowing When" Photo- This is a photo of me when I struggled with insomnia. I have since overcome it through writing & healing the broken parts of myself.

"Daylight Savings"- The italicized words are song to a sweet melody I created. It is a fun piece to perform. It reflects the overcoming of a bad relationship through self love.

"Soul Filled" Photo- This beautiful woman is *Jamala Milele Lott*, she so graciously provided her photo to me when I reached out for a "beauty-full figured woman" to compliment my haiku. She owns all copyrights to this photo and others throughout manuscript. You can check her works & thoughts at http://confessionsofa.webs.com/confessions.htm.

"To You"- Read the poem as is, then read by reading only the bold words. I enjoyed reading both ways, hope you the reader will too!

"Night Out" Photo- Two of my wonderful friends, I like to call sisters, *Jeneta Tunnell & Amber Milliner* (back to camera). Photo taken by yours truly, Fall of 2009 in Fayetteville, NC at a night club.

Second Blossom: Watering The Seed

"Computer Sense" Photo- Photo provided by Natasha L. Guy

"Dream of a Nation"- The first stanza has a quote italicized which is by *David L. Blackwell*. He gave me this beautiful thought when I asked him to provide a word of encouragement for me to place on my "wall of wisdom". I appreciate him and his friendship.

"Tobacco Burn"- Some of you may have already guessed this, but while editing, I decided to make the poem appear like a burning cigarette. Did you not notice? Go back and view it.

"America- Land of the Homeless" Poet Da Champ- This poet is the founder of LoveLifePain Productions. I am honored to know him as a fellow poet and friend. His work takes his listeners and readers by storm. Never afraid of any mic; he is truly an accomplished artist. You can check out his album: "Da Streets Need A Prophet" and more on his websites.
http://www.dachamp.net/;
http://www.wix.com/da_champ/llpproductions &
http://dachampdapoet.bandcamp.com/.

"America- Land of the Homeless"- This poem was written as one poem though it has two very important situations that fall under the same category, which is homelessness. The first section, written by myself, is based off a true story of a couple living in the woods of Asheville, NC (as seen on news). The second section, written by Da Champ, refers to a friend who experienced the harsh reality of Hurricane Katrina.

"According to Church Folks"- The italicized words are from the Negro spiritual "Changed My Name". Please note there are different variations to this song. Check out www.negrospirituals.com.

"Blaq Majik" Photo- This is a black & white photo of a painting, or Luvleeh Doodle, I did in 2010 for *Luvleeh Inks & Links*.

"Sequence" Photo- This is the casket of a loved one. Rest in peace E.P.M.

"Blind Theories"- I give credit where it is due; and my wonderful friend *Barron Davis* provided the name of this poem for me. I thought it captured everything I wrote about within the piece.

Third Blossom: The Stories Untold

"Take Me There" Poet Brandon McCoy- This poet though young, has accomplished much in the poetry world. He has a distinct way of capturing the mind of his readers with the depths of his imagery and content. For more info see www.poetrypoem.com/flyyoungman or email: mr_mccoy2004@yahoo.com.

"Gem In Eye"- This poem is about my sister/friend & *Poet Gemynii Evolving*. She took a picture lying across a dock that I came across, which sparked the poem. She is an accomplished poet in her own right showcasing across the tri-state Carolina area, featured in artist magazines and more. She is also the author of the poem I respond to in "Undeniable Lust". Her style is both unique and eccentric. Thus, she is truly a Gem In Eye~ Check out her works on FB: Gemynii Evolving or follow her on Twitter: @GemyniiEvolving.

"Gypsy Dove"- This poem is about my sister, artist, jeweler, sculptor & writer -*Annastaysia Savage*, & her gypsy heritage. She truly has given me the open door to the arts by supporting me, the artist behind Luvleeh Inks & Links. I thank her for her love and support.

"Hush Little Baby"- the italicized words are from the famous lullaby/ classic nursery rhyme.

"Warm Innocence of The Spring"- Previously printed in the 2005-2006 edition of literary journal: *The Phoenix* at Elizabeth City State University, in which I was a contributing editor.

"She Speaks" Photo- This photo is of my mother *Consuelo D. Hill*, circa 1970's while attending Virginia State University.

"Undeniable Lust"- see "Gem In Eye"

"Echoes Against A Brick Wall" Photo- This is again *Jamala Milele Lott*. She owns all copyrights to this photo. Permission provided for use.

"Her Eyes" Photo- This is again my sister *Jeneta Tunnell*, who so graciously let me use her photo for this book. She is truly a representation of the many goddesses in my life.

"Without A Word"- Italicized words are from Beyonce's song "Speechless".

"Sun Kissed" Photo- My friend *Barron Davis* & I

"Apologies"- Italicized words are from Jill Scott's song "Comes to the Light".

Who is Luvleeh Poetiklocks?

"Vinroy Reid"- Founder of Youth H.O.P.E. International Inc. A non-profit organization based in Charlotte N.C to aid with the growth & involvement of the community with the youth. Check out information on the Youth Hope International Center, Charlotte, NC.

If you are in need of an editor please contact: LeighLambEditor@gmail.com

Please note chapbooks mentioned are *limited edition prints*.

Made in the USA
Columbia, SC
19 May 2024

35478455R00085